Incredible Manatees

Exploring Our Incredible World Series

By **Mark Smith**

Copyright 2012 All Rights Reserved

Check Out More Great Animal Adventures At

www.OurIncredibleWorld.com

ISBN-13: 978-1494436162
ISBN-10: 1494436167

Table of Contents

Incredible Manatees...1
A Message From the Author..3
What Is A Manatee?..4
What Do Manatees Eat?..13
Where Do Manatees Live?..17
Manatee Babies...18
Are Manatees Important?...19
Amazing Manatee Facts...20
Are There Different Types of Manatees?..........................22
An Incredible Manatee Experience!..................................25
More Cool Manatee Pictures..28

A Message From the Author

I have been lucky enough to have several encounters with manatees throughout my life, and they have all been amazing. If I learned anything from my encounters with this incredible animal, it would have to be this. Manatees are extremely friendly, and they almost seem to enjoy interactions with people. This is one of the few animals on our planet that will look you right in the eye, and you feel an instant connection. You quickly realize that the manatee has been smiling at you the entire time, and you can't help but smile back.

They are incredibly curious animals. They want to know what is going on around them almost all the time. I am thankful for the experiences that I have had with these wonderful creatures. I will tell you a little more about these experiences in just a little bit, but let's take a closer look at the awesome manatee first.

What Is A Manatee?

Take a good look at this manatee. What is the first thing you think of when you look at it? You are probably saying, "Wow! I have never seen anything like that!" Most people have not. Manatees are not something you see walking down the middle of the street, and most zoos or animal parks don't have them on display either.

Did you happen to notice that the manatee does not have any legs or arms. This creature has flippers.

What Is A Manatee?

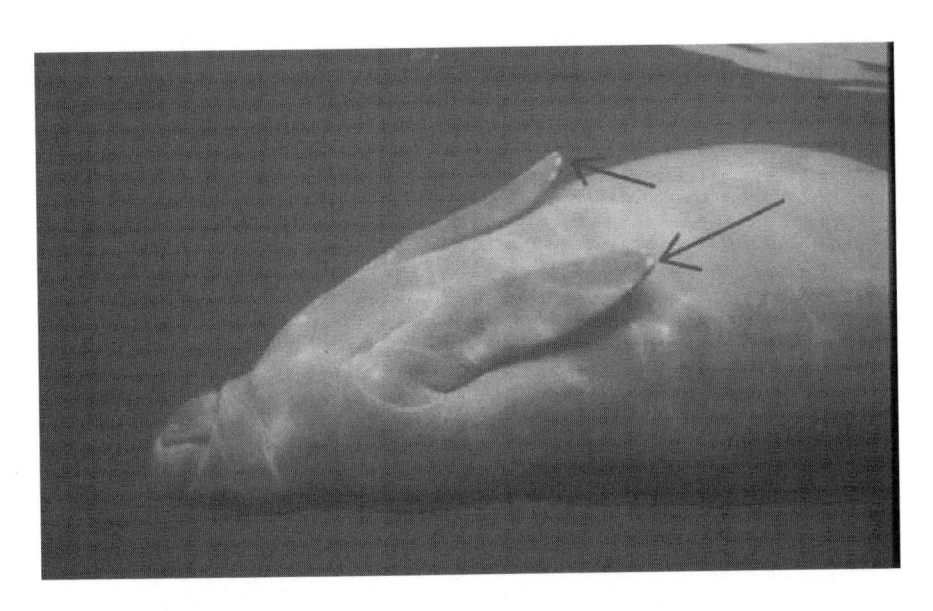

This manatee is being silly. It has decided to swim upside down. Sometimes manatees do that. If you were to look very closely at a manatee's flippers, you would see they have fingernails.

Their flippers almost look like an elephants foot that has been squished. That is because elephants and manatees are closely related. You could think of them as cousins.

What else do you see when you look at the manatee? Do you see that big tail? At the end of the manatee's tail is a big flipper. They use this flipper to propel them through the water. The manatee tail reminds me of one of the incredible experiences that I had with a manatee when I was a boy.

When I was younger, my father would take my older brother and I out on his big sailboat. I was about 10 or 12 years old at the time. We would live on his sailboat for weeks at a time. One of our favorite spots to go happened to be a small group of islands in Florida. Manatees loved swimming in the shallow waters around all of these islands. We got to see them all the time.

One day while we were playing in the water close to one of the islands, a group of manatees came in close. The water was shallow so I could quietly walk up to the manatees and get a close look. I wanted to see if I could reach out and touch one of them.

I was very quiet as I approached them. I took little tiny baby steps. They were right next to me in the water. They did not even know that I was standing there. I could reach out and touch them. I took one step closer, and I scared the manatee that was closest to me. It flipped its giant tail up, and when it did, the manatee's tail hit me right in the back of my leg. The power from that tail lifted me out of the water, and flipped me over.

When I stood back up, the manatees were gone, and my leg was hurting. I walked out of the water on shaky legs. I looked down at the back of my leg where the manatee tail had hit me, and there was a bruise about the size of a baseball on the back of my leg. It was huge.

The manatee did not mean to hurt me. I got too close and scared the manatee. It was just trying to get away! I remember explaining that bruise to all my friends in school the following week. What an incredible experience!

What Is A Manatee?

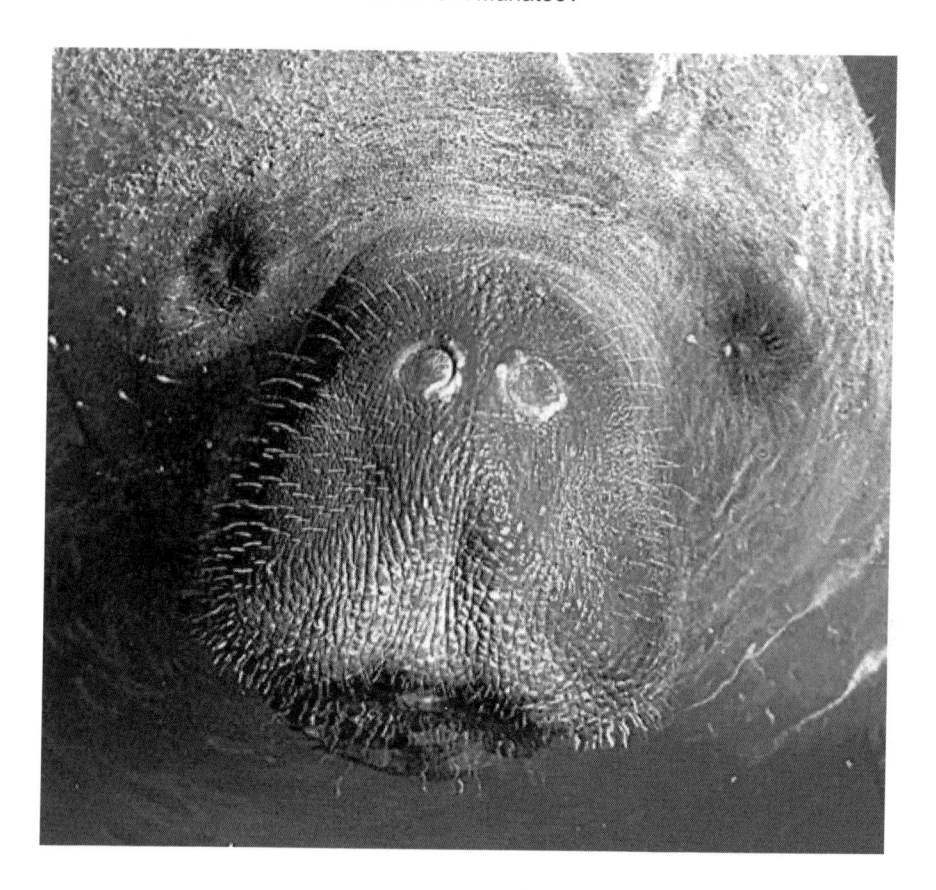

Let's take a closer look at the manatee's face. Can you see all of the little hairs all over the manatee's face. These feel like a brush. These are the manatee's whiskers.

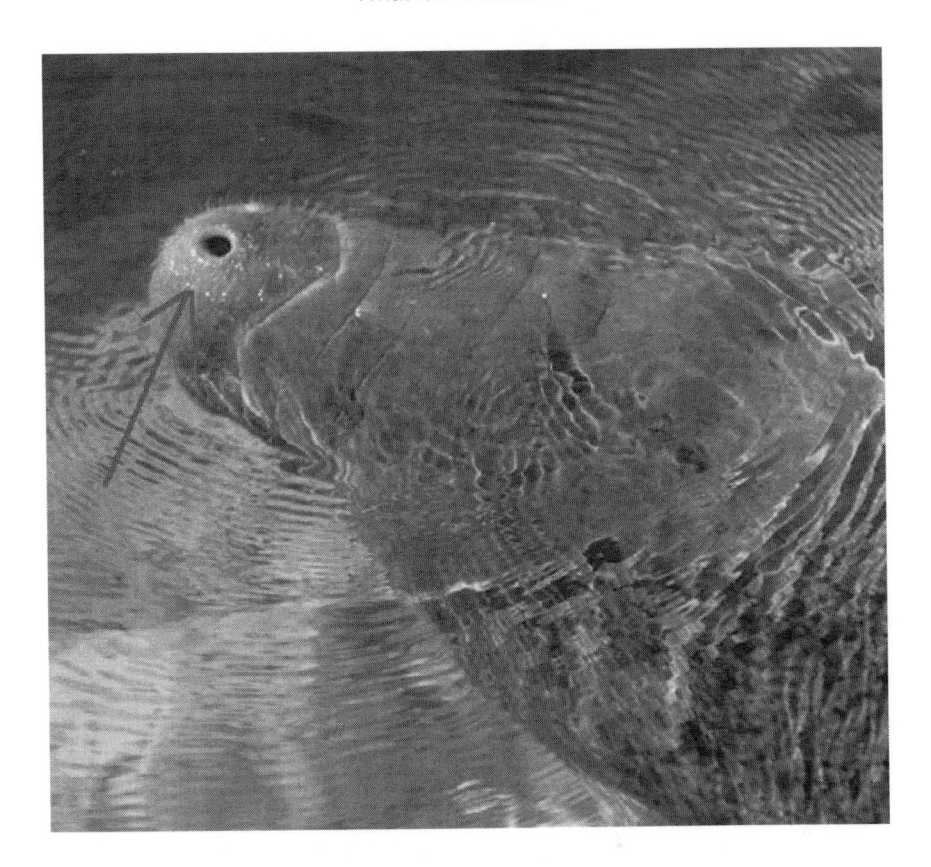

Can you see the manatee's nose? A manatee does not use its nose for smelling. It will use its nose to breathe air. That's right! Manatees breathe air just like you and me. They will come up to the surface of the water, take a big deep breath with their noses, and dive back down.

Manatees are mammals. This means that they breathe air just like you and me. They have warm blood just like you and me and they give birth to live young. Aren't manatees incredible?

Do manatees have ears?
Manatees don't have ears like we do, but they can hear very well. It is really difficult to see their ears. They are just a tiny little dimple located behind their eyes.

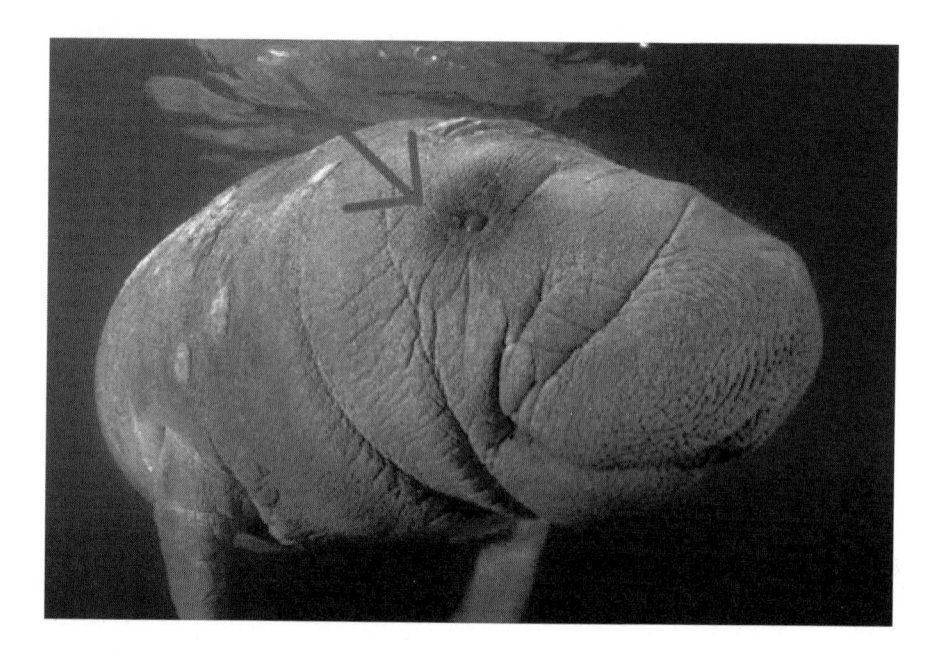

Do manatees have eyes?

Manatees do have eyes, but they don't have any eyelids. In order for a manatee to close its eyes, it uses the muscles around its eyes to kind of squish the skin around its eye.

Do manatees have teeth?

They certainly do! Manatees have molars in the back of their mouths that help them crush their food. Their teeth have been nicknamed, "Marching Molars" because they are constantly being replaced. New teeth will grow in the back of the mouth and slowly move forward throughout their lives. As the teeth move forward, they will slowly wear down from all of the things they eat. It is like a very slow conveyor belt of teeth. That is pretty cool!

Look at this manatee's back. It is covered in weeds! This is normal. Sometimes aquatic plants grow on a manatee's back.

What Do Manatees Eat?

Manatees are herbivores. This means that they will only eat plants, and since these gentle giants live in the water, they only eat aquatic plants. They can be seen eating plants that live at the bottom, plants that float around on the surface and they have even been known to eat plants that are growing on the shore. They will stick their heads out of the water and munch on the plants that are growing on the shore. Some manatees have even been seen eating acorns from tree branches that hang low in the water.

Manatees have also been known to drink from freshwater hoses at docks and boat ramps.

This reminds me of another encounter that I had with a manatee. My son and I were at a state park in Florida called Blue Spring.

Blue Spring is a large freshwater spring. The water in the spring is always 72.5 degrees and it is usually crystal clear. It is an amazing place to see with a mask and snorkel. You will see large schools of fish, turtles and the occasional otter.

The water flows out of the spring and into the St. John's River. It is estimated that millions of gallons of water flow out of the spring every single day.

It was a hot summer afternoon, and my son and I had the place to ourselves. The water was shallow enough for me to walk, but my son was swimming next to me with his mask and snorkel. I was keeping an eye out while we made our way down the spring run. I have seen alligators in the area so I thought it would be a good idea to look ahead while my son snorkeled around me.

We were about halfway down the spring run when I spotted a large dark shape out of the corner of my eye. It was coming right for us. For a split second I was scared. I thought that a large alligator was coming right towards me and my son. I reached down in the water and grabbed my son by the shoulder and pulled him up in my arms. It was at that exact moment that I realized the large dark shape was a manatee.

I put my son back in the water, and the manatee swam right up to us. The manatee was busy eating plants on the bottom of the spring run. It circled us a few times and swam up to my son for a closer look. They looked at each other for a second, and then the manatee continued to eat.

Later that evening my son told me that the manatee was like a vacuum cleaner. It was just swimming along the bottom sucking up all the weeds that it could find. That was an incredible experience.

Manatees love Blue Spring, but only in the winter. When the waters of the St Johns river start to get cold, manatees by the hundreds will swim into the spring. It is an incredible site to see. People come from all over the world to watch the manatees swimming in the water. During the winter, the spring becomes a manatee refuge. You are not allowed to swim in the water when all the manatees are there.

That day my son and I were there, it was the middle of the summer. We were very lucky to get a close up view of this incredible creature.

Where Do Manatees Live?

You can only find manatees in a very few places on our planet. This species of animal is currently endangered. This means that there are not many of them left. There are laws that now protect the manatees. In Florida it is against the law to disturb the manatee in any way.

You can find manatees in Florida and along the coastline of Florida. You can also find manatees in the Amazon, the Gulf coast of the United States, the Caribbean, South America and Africa.

Manatee Babies

A female manatee will be pregnant for about a year. When the baby manatee is born, it is one of the cutest animals on the planet. A female manatee will give birth to just one baby. Baby manatees are called calves, and they will depend on their mothers to teach them everything that they need to survive.

The manatee calf will stay with its mother for up to two years. During those two years, the mother manatee will teach her baby how to swim and eat. She will also teach her calf how to find the best places for food and shelter.

A baby manatee will nurse for about three months. The mother manatee produces milk for her calf just like other mammals.

Are Manatees Important?

Every animal on our planet is very important, including the manatee. Animals help keep things in balance.

Manatees are a very important part of the food chain. They help keep plant levels under control, and all of the plants that they do eat help provide nutrients and fertilizer to other creatures in the water.

Manatees are very important creatures, but they are currently an endangered species. There are not very many of them left on our planet. Thankfully they have been protected.

Manatees face several challenges in their life. The biggest challenge that they need to overcome is cold weather. They can't survive in cold weather conditions. This is why you can find manatees searching for warmer waters in the winter months. If they can't escape the cold water, they will die.

Manatees also have the challenge of trying to avoid all of the motor boats. Motor boats move faster than the manatee, and they will often collide with the manatee. In Florida, there are special areas in lakes, oceans and rivers where motor boats have to drive very slowly. These are called manatee, or no wake zones. When motor boats travel slowly, it gives the manatee time to move out of the way.

Amazing Manatee Facts

Did you know that the manatee is also called the "sea cow?" The manatee is not related to the cow in any way. People have give the manatee the nickname of "sea cow" because it is so big.

When manatees were first seen by people, they were believed to be mermaids. Christopher Columbus saw three manatees when he arrived in America. He thought the manatees were mermaids. Does that look like a mermaid to you?

Manatees don't have feet, but they leave a footprint in the water. When a manatee swims, it uses its large tail to move it through the water. Their tail leaves a large bubble like circle in the water. If you are looking down in the water, you can see this circle appearing every time the manatee moves its large tail. This is called the manatee's footprint.

Manatees can live to be 60 years old!

A full grown manatee can weigh as much as 1200 pounds or 550 kilos.

A manatee will eat about 110 pounds or 50 kilos of food every day.

A manatee can hold its breath for about 15 minutes.

Manatees spend about half of their day sleeping.

Are There Different Types of Manatees?

There are currently three confirmed species of manatee. The most common is the West Indian Manatee. This manatee is actually divided into two different sub-species. There is the Florida manatee that lives almost exclusively in Florida, and there is the Antillean Manatee which can be found in Florida, the Gulf of Mexico, Texas, the Caribbean, Mexico and some portions of South America. Here is a map that shows where this species of manatee lives.

West Indian Manatee Range

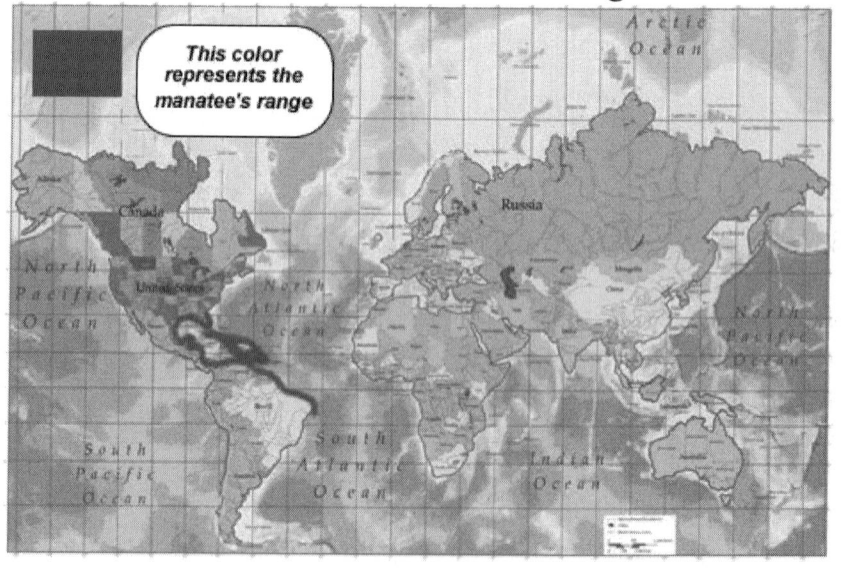

This color represents the manatee's range

West African Manatee

This just might be the rarest manatee in the world. At the time of this writing, very little was known about the West African Manatee. Scientists have not been able to fully study this species of manatee just yet. They suspect that it is very similar to the West Indian Manatee.

West African Manatee Range

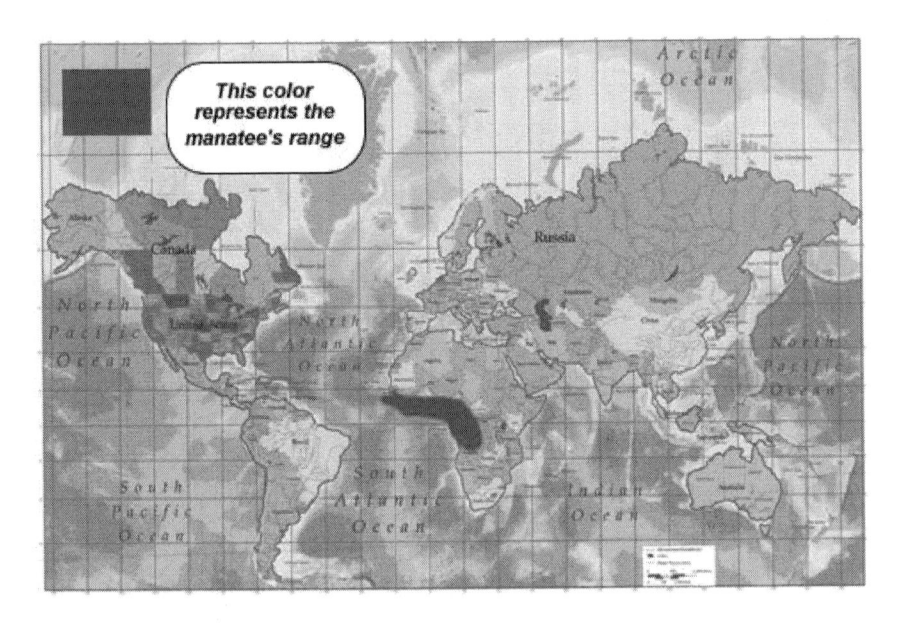

Amazonian Manatee

This species of Manatee calls the Amazon river home, and they are smaller than the other two manatees mentioned above. This species of manatee never ventures out to the sea.

Amazonian Manatee Range

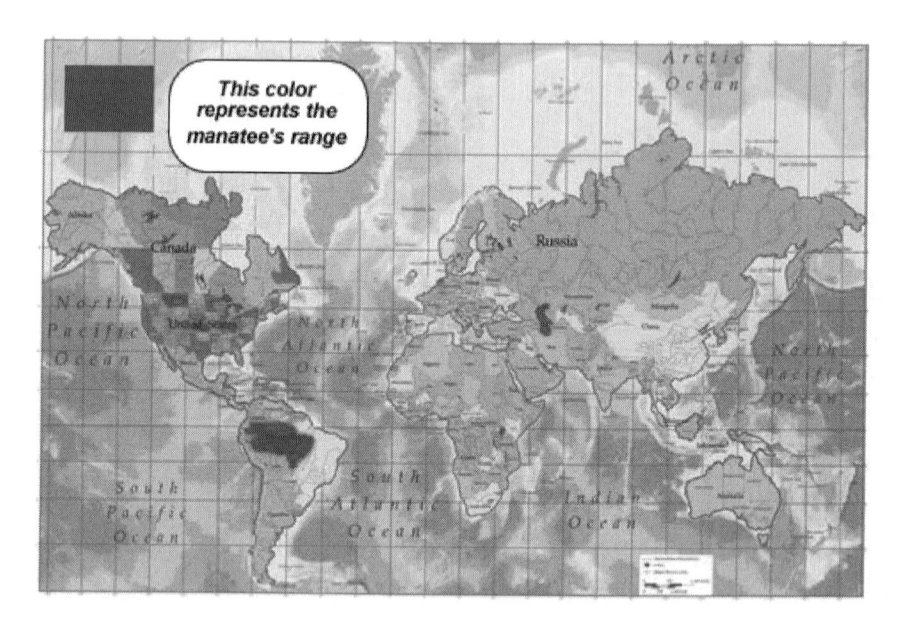

An Incredible Manatee Experience!

I did save my favorite manatee experience for last. It happened one summer afternoon while my brother and I were out fishing in a really neat place called Mosquito Lagoon. Can you guess why they called it that? When the sun went down, this place came to life with mosquitoes. They were everywhere.

Mosquito Lagoon is a large area of brackish water in Florida. Brackish water is a mixture of fresh and salt water. This is one of the best places to fish in Florida, and it is also a really good place to see some great wildlife.

My brother and I found what we thought would be a good spot to fish. Our little spot was tucked away behind a couple of islands. The water was only about 4 feet or 1.2 meters deep. I anchored my boat, and we both started fishing.

Neither one of us were having any luck fishing, and we both decided that it was time to go. I walked around to the back of my boat to lower the motor into the water. I lowered the motor into the water, and a manatee surfaced right at the back of my boat. I was a little surprised to see a manatee come so close to my boat. It swam right up to the back of my motor and started nuzzling the motor with its mouth. The motor was not on, so it could not hurt the manatee. I couldn't believe my eyes. I lifted the motor back out of the water, and walked around the side of my boat to get my brother.

An Incredible Manatee Experience!

I said, "Hey, come look at this manatee right at the back of the boat." He walked around the back.

"Good one Mark. There is no manatee back here." said my brother.

I looked over the side of the boat, and the manatee surfaced right at my feet. I yelled to my brother, "It is over here now. Come check this out!"

The manatee stuck its head out of the water and looked right at me. There it was. It was just staring at me. I slowly kneeled down to get a better look at this curious manatee. As soon as I got close enough to touch the manatee, it did something absolutely amazing. It rolled over on its back, and stuck its flippers out of the water. By this time my brother had made his way over to the side of the boat.

I looked up and my brother and said, "I think it wants me to scratch its belly."

I reached down, and the manatee slowly grabbed my hand with its flippers. It pulled my hand down to its belly. It wanted me to scratch and pet its belly. I could not believe what was happening. I started rubbing and scratching its belly, and the manatee would occasionally roll over and look me right in the eye. It would then roll back over, grab my hand and pull it to its belly again. My brother and I were completely in awe. Here we were out in the middle of this large body of water. There were no people or houses for miles, and this manatee wanted us to reach down and scratch its belly. This is an amazing experience that I will remember for the rest of my life.

After a little while, the manatee swam away from our boat. I still could not believe what had happened. I pulled up the anchor, and looked around for the manatee. I could not see it anywhere. I knew that it was still close by, so I pushed my boat into deeper water with a paddle.

When we got to deeper water, I looked back over my shoulder to see if I could spot the manatee one more time. What I saw next completely blew me away. In the distance I saw the manatee's flipper come out of the water like it was waving at me. I waved back and went on my way. My brother and I were very fortunate to have this great experience, and I am happy to have shared it with you. Maybe someday you will get to see a manatee in person. I really hope you do because they are incredible animals!

More Cool Manatee Pictures

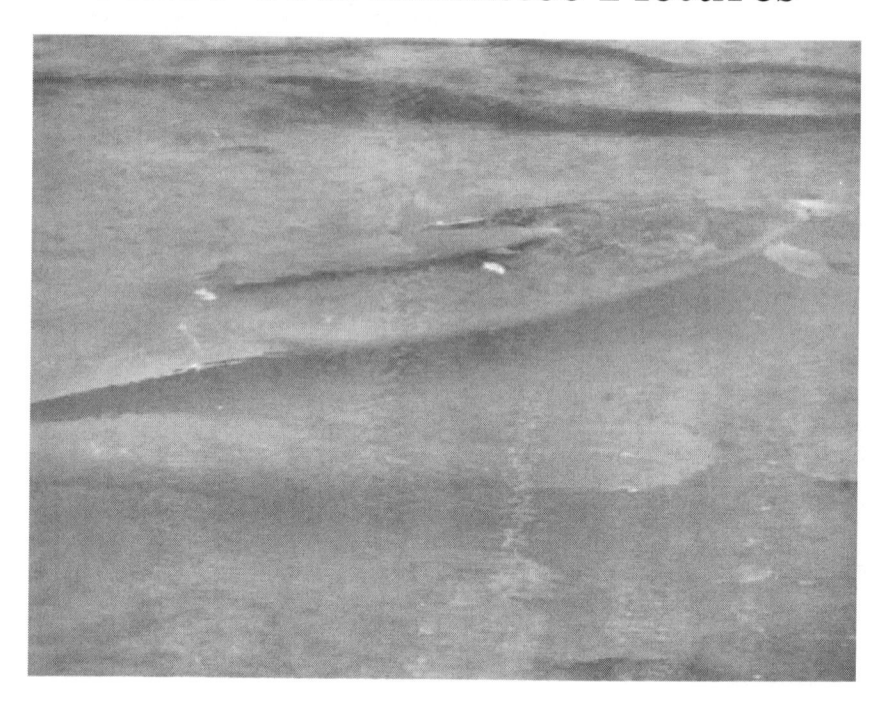

More Cool Manatee Pictures

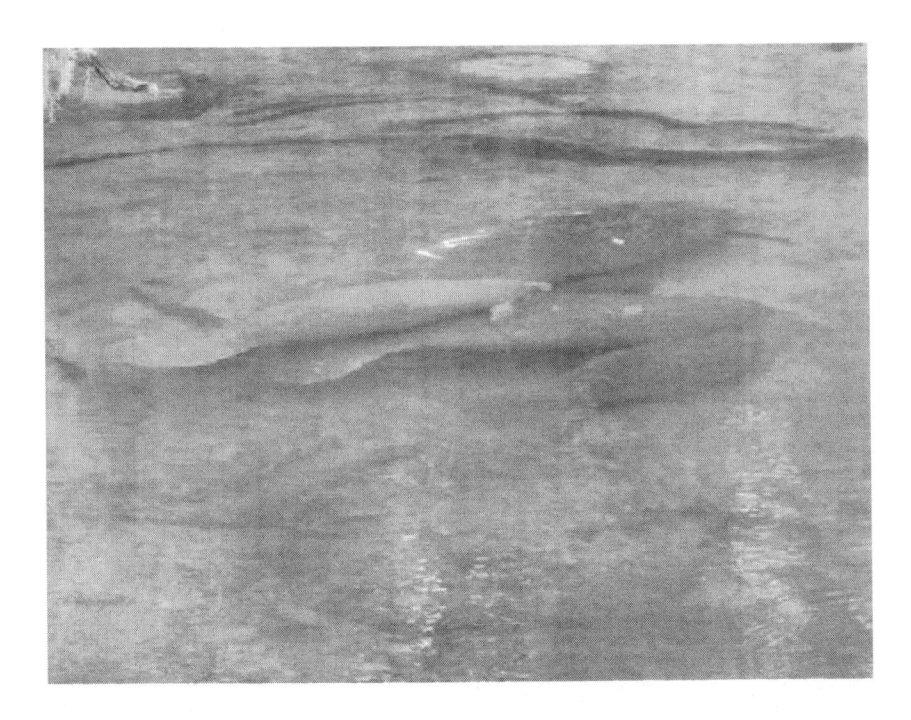

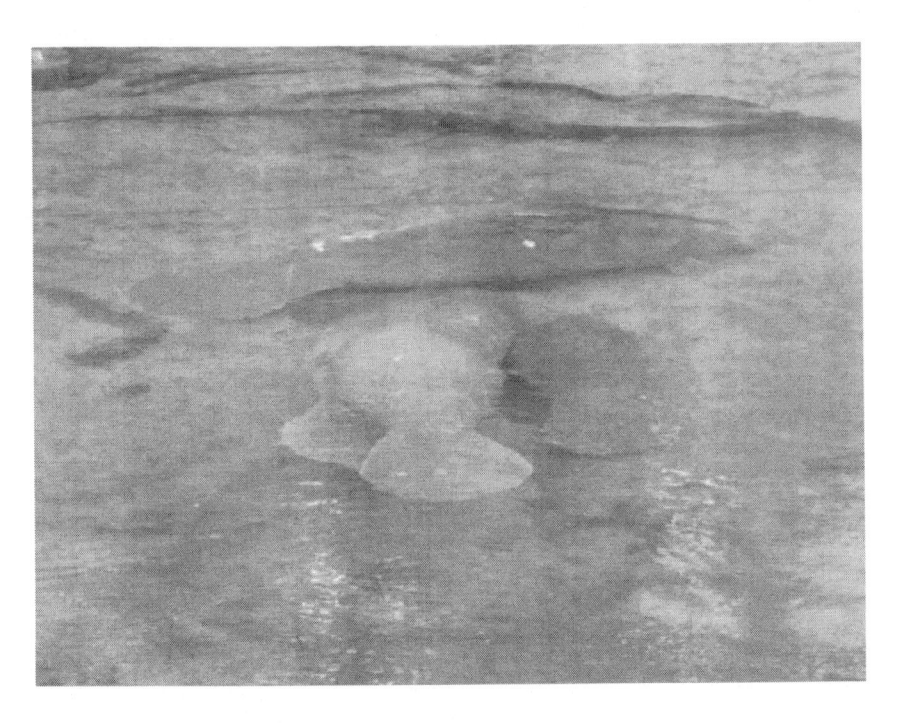

More Cool Manatee Pictures

More Cool Manatee Pictures

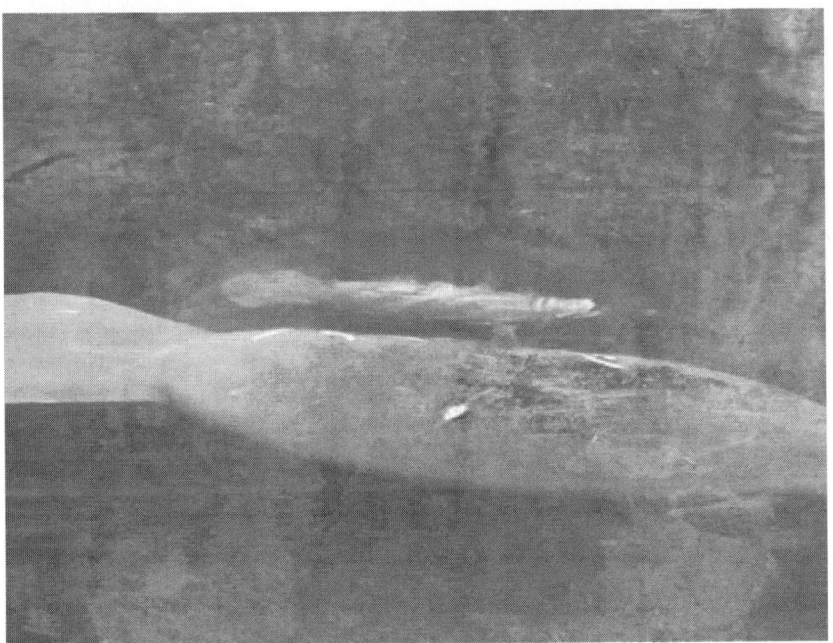

More Cool Manatee Pictures

Thank you so much for purchasing this book! I really hope you enjoyed your adventure, but more importantly I hope that you learned something about Our Incredible World.

Printed in Great Britain
by Amazon.co.uk, Ltd.,
Marston Gate.